P9-EEJ-881

Sports Illustrated
BASKETBALL

The Sports Illustrated Library

BOOKS ON TEAM SPORTS

Baseball	Football: Defense	Ice Hockey
Basketball	Football: Offense	Soccer
Curling: Techniques	Football: Quarterback	Volleyball
and Strategy		

BOOKS ON INDIVIDUAL SPORTS

Badminton	Horseback Riding	Table Tennis
Fly Fishing	Judo	Tennis
Golf	Skiing	Track: Running Events
Handball	Squash	

BOOKS ON WATER SPORTS

| Powerboating | Small Boat Sailing |
| Skin Diving and Snorkeling | Swimming and Diving |

SPECIAL BOOKS

| Dog Training | Training with Weights |
| Safe Driving | |

Sports Illustrated
BASKETBALL

BY THE EDITORS OF
SPORTS ILLUSTRATED

J. B. LIPPINCOTT COMPANY
PHILADELPHIA AND NEW YORK
1971

The opening section of Chapter 2, pages 29–31, is reprinted in slightly revised form from "U.C.L.A.: Simple, Awesomely Simple," by Curry Kirkpatrick, in *Sports Illustrated*, November 30, 1970.

ISBN-0-397-00881-3 Cloth Edition
ISBN-0-397-00882-1 Paper Edition

Copyright © 1956, 1957, 1958, 1960, 1961, 1962, 1970, 1971 by Time Inc.
All rights reserved
Revised Edition
NINTH PRINTING
Printed in the United States of America
Library of Congress Catalog Card Number: 76–168552

Photographs from *Sports Illustrated*, © Time Inc.
Cover photograph: John G. Zimmerman
Photograph on page 10: *Neil Leifer*
Photograph on page 28: *James Drake*
Photographs on pages 38 and 88: *Sheedy & Long*
Photograph on page 70: *Leviton–Atlanta*

CAMROSE LUTHERAN COLLEGE LIBRARY

GV
885
.578

24,104

Preface

LET us begin with the blunt fact that reading this book will not turn you into a good basketball player. Pete Maravich once admitted to having a certain edge over other boys because his father was a coach, but he quickly pointed out that it was practice—hours of it—that made him the great player he is. And so it must be with you. In this book you will find basics of offense and defense, a description of the Wooden Way—the great UCLA's coach's method of producing championship teams—a lesson on how to work the zone press and, finally, a tribute to Bob Cousy, that legendary Celtic. But the work of becoming a better player is up to you. We only hope this book will make your task easier and more fun.

Contents

Text by Dudley Moore with Gwilym Brown
Drawings by Daniel Schwartz

Text by Curry Kirkpatrick and John R. Wooden

Text by Dudley Moore with Gwilym Brown
Drawings by Ed Vebell

Text by William Leggett
Drawings by Shelley Fink

Text by Arlie W. Schardt
Drawings by Ed Vebell

Text by Dudley Moore with Gwilym Brown
Drawings by Robert Riger

Preface and Text Revisions by Walter Bingham

Sports Illustrated
BASKETBALL

1
Defense:
Some Simple Pointers

THE BASIC STANCE

THE starting point from which to teach defensive basketball is the stance. Many coaches advocate the so-called boxer
stance (Figure 1) because it allows the defender to cover a
greater amount of area, quickly, than any other. One foot is
well forward. It doesn't really matter which, except when an
opponent is being guarded along the side or end lines; then
the forward foot must be the one nearest to the line to cut
off that side as a possible driving lane. The other foot is
back. The weight is evenly distributed on the balls of both
feet, though the heels are still in contact with the floor. The
body is bent at the waist and the knees well flexed to
maintain a good, aggressive position. The forward hand is
raised and extended toward the opponent to harry and upset
him as well as block his vision. The other hand is held at
waist level, poised to block the passing lane on that side.

Figure 1

Now, when the opponent drives toward the basket, the defender is ready for him. If his man goes to his right (Figure 2) defender pivots off his left foot, taking a quick step back (arrow) along the path of the drive with his right foot, his right hand reaching out to cut off a possible pass or dribble. If his opponent moves to his left (Figure 3), the defender pivots off his right foot, takes a long step back along the path of the drive with the left (arrow), swinging his left hand down into the lane to deflect a possible pass.

12

Figure 2

Figure 3

THE VITAL FLOOR POSITION

Under most circumstances when guarding a man without the ball the defender should always stay between his man and the basket. In Figure 4, the defender is devoting close attention to his man, but is also keeping an eye on the ball. If the ball is moved away from his man, he will "sag off," dropping back a little toward the basket to help jam up the middle lane. If the ball is moved into the area near his man, he must then move up closer, almost in direct proportion to the distance his man is from the ball. In the critical scoring area within fifteen feet of the basket, the defender abandons this principle in favor of aggressively playing the ball.

Figure 4

Figure 5

In Figure 5, an offensive player cuts toward the basket, but the defender, instead of staying behind him (and nearer the basket) moves in front of his opponent, trying to beat him to the desired position. The pass to the cutter under the basket must now be lobbed over the defender's

head, a difficult trick, and it can often be blocked or inter-cepted. The risk involved in this tactic is that the defender may allow his man to get too far in back of him and thus be an easy target for a pass. The gamble is worth taking be-cause a challenging defense pays off more often than not.

17

Figure 6

STOPPING THE PIVOT MAN

Trying to stop a good, big pivot man who takes up a position along the foul lane is one of the toughest defensive assignments a team can be asked to handle. The most effective way is to see that he doesn't get the ball too often, mainly by blocking off the passing lanes.

In Figure 6, the player (No. 10) assigned to guard the pivot man should play alongside and slightly in front of him. As the offensive team passes the ball from one side of the court to the other, the defender crosses over behind the pivot man if he is out by the foul line, and in front if he is closer to the basket. This makes it more difficult for the offensive team to feed the ball to the pivot. Another defensive player (right) helps out by sagging-off his own man, alert to protect against a pass which may be lobbed to the pivot man if he turns away from the defender and toward the basket, or to help tie him up if he does get the ball. It is evident that this means risking the possibility that the third opponent (right) may receive the ball and have a clear outside shot, but this is far better than letting the pivot man have an easy close-in shot.

Figure 7

THE TIME TO GAMBLE

An extremely significant part of tight defense is a readiness to take risks in actually going for the ball when the occasion arises. This is the real meaning of aggressive defense. Players should neglect their assigned men when they feel certain of being able to pull off a successful steal, intercept a dribble or pass or, at least, tie up the ball.

20

In Figure 7, a defensive man, realizing that he has an excellent chance to succeed, has ignored his own man in an attempt to steal the ball from another offensive player. Even if he doesn't actually get possession, he will surely stall the opposition's plans by causing a jump ball. At the very worst, he has neglected a player who doesn't have the ball and so cannot score.

THE SWITCH IS FUNDAMENTAL

The sudden changing of defensive assignments, known as switching, is a basic part of man-to-man defense. It is used to circumvent the blocks and screens set up by the offense. Figures 8A and B, involving a pivot man stationed at the foul line, show a typical switching situation. The player with the ball dribbles directly in front of his teammate, so that the defender on the right is blocked off (8A). Defender No. 34, since he must now shift to the ball, calls "Switch!" and moves quickly away from his man to pick up the dribbler (8B).

A

Figure 8

Meanwhile, No. 12 is now responsible for No. 11 and must move around him (arrow) as quickly as possible to protect against a pass from the man who still has the ball. Even if there is now an unequal height alignment on defense (as shown in 8B), this switch should be maintained until it is safe to return to the original assignments. This kind of aggressive switching to the ball very often leads to a steal, and is especially effective in the critical scoring area close to the basket.

B

THE BLOCK-OUT FOR REBOUNDS

The defensive men must hold their proper positions as the ball leaves the shooter's hands (see Figure 9A). They wait until their men have begun to commit themselves for the rebound on particular paths toward the basket. Then they take quick cross-over steps into those paths (see arrow in Figure 9B), blocking out the offensive players. Having jockeyed into position between their opponents and the basket, they hold them off with their backs while facing toward the impending rebound (Figure 9B). The trick is for each defender to avoid being forced in too close under the backboard, where the ball could rebound out over his head—a common error even among the pros.

The defensive men should maintain position, crouched and ready to leap upward, with the opponents blocked out, until they are certain that they have timed the often erratic rebound correctly. A step ahead of their men, they should then go in and up for the ball, which should be grasped securely in both hands, not batted away.

Figure 9   A

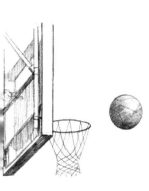

B

Figure 10

THE FAILURE TO PIVOT

A common error by the defender often occurs when the offensive player starts to drive around him and he takes a short sideward step instead of a deep back pivot step (page 13). In Figure 10A, above, the defender has just done this (arrow) and is off balance. As a result, his opponent is given a driving lane to the basket and the only way the defender can stop him is to foul him. The defensive man in Figure 10B, however, has first pivoted correctly (arrow), thus containing the dribbler and cutting off the direct lane to the basket.

26

THE USELESS LEAP

A common offensive tactic is to fake a shot, watch the defender soar into the air in a premature attempt to block it, and then dribble neatly around him for two easy points. In order to avoid this mistake, players should never leave their feet to block a shot unless the opponent has used up his dribble. Of course, if an opponent is starting to score from outside, the guard must close in even though the opponent may successfully drive around him; here he can expect help from a teammate. If a man is going to beat you with his outside shooting, you've got to force him into doing something else.

Another common mistake: as a general rule a defender should not cross one leg over the other in trying to stay with his man. He must always slide the forward foot out first and then step with the trailing foot.

Figure 11

2

The UCLA System and the Zone Defense

THE WOODEN WAY

ANYONE interested in playing better basketball would do well to study the methods of John Wooden, whose UCLA Bruins have now won five straight NCAA championships and seven in the last eight years. The UCLA system—Wooden's system—is founded on the simple basics of conditioning, fundamentals, and teamwork which, admirable qualities though they may be, are only goals for other teams. At UCLA, they are necessities.

The UCLA way is hammered into a new player almost from the very first day. In practice and games a player must acknowledge a good pass from a teammate. If he doesn't do this, he doesn't play. Among Wooden's other "normal expectations," which are presented to each player at the beginning of the season, are: he must never criticize, "nag or razz" at teammate; never be selfish, jealous, envious, or egotistical; never "grandstand, loaf, sulk, or boast"; never

29

"have reason to be sorry afterward." There are other expressions of the UCLA way too.

Shooting: Wooden determines the area from which a player is accurate, and he is restricted to that area. A Henry Bibby, for instance, could shoot from 25 feet but not from 10 feet after a cut inside, where a John Vallely could. Wooden will change a man's form if he either cannot get the shot off or cannot hit it when he does shoot.

Passing: UCLA players look not for the man but for a spot on the man—his shoulder, his extended arm. Also, to avoid blindside fouling, they screen spots on the floor instead of opponents.

Rebounding: Wooden teaches his men to: (1) assume any shot will be missed, (2) get their hands up the moment any shot is taken, and (3) step in front of the opponent and go for the ball. "Blocking out is negative rebounding," he says. "We charge the ball."

In addition to everything else, the Bruins are constantly running. All conditioning drills are competitive, and UCLA teams work just as hard on fundamentals during the last week of a season as during the first. Wooden still preserves the practice plan for each day that he has coached at UCLA and he brings to the daily sessions a 3-by-5-inch card with notations of what to do each minute in order that he not forget. "His cards", mutters one current player. "He drives me crazy with his damn cards."

Despite their moaning, UCLA players know they are ready after a week of seemingly endless drills. "They are ready for the pros too," said Mike Harren of the '67 and '68 champions. "That's why UCLA guys get through rookie camp so easily. They've got the fundamentals down. If a man wants to play pro ball, there's only one man to play for in college—Wooden."

THE UCLA ZONE PRESS

Think of Wooden and UCLA and most people think of

that swarming defense known as the zone press.

The press is not the exclusive property of UCLA, but it has been the Bruins, beginning with the 1964 team, who have showed fans how devastating and effective the press can be. "The two-minute explosion" is what John Underwood of *Sports Illustrated* called it as UCLA, pressing Duke late in the first half, scored sixteen straight points to ice the game and give Coach Wooden his first NCAA title. "What makes UCLA super," Underwood wrote, "is the deadly art of self-defense Wooden teaches, and you can not imagine how offensive defense can be until you have seen UCLA's busters gang up on the backboard or on some taller team."

The next few pages tell, in Wooden's own words, how the UCLA press works.* He uses his first championship team as an example.

The 1964 UCLA team, which went through the season without a loss in thirty games and finished the season by winning the NCAA championship despite the fact that in this day of very tall men they had no starter over 6 feet, 5 inches, used a two-two-one zone press defense with remarkable effectiveness.

This particular defense was used for several reasons. First, I thought the individual talents of the starting personnel fitted it very well; second, some method was needed in this West Coast area of ball-control teams to prevent our fast-break–minded boys from being lulled into a slow tempo; third, I thought our quickness would enable us to play this type of defense quite well; and, fourth, I felt that this type of game would help to neutralize the advantage in height that all of our opponents would have.

Furthermore, I must point out that this type of defense was not designed to take the ball away from the opposition nearly as much as to force them into mental and physical errors on which we hoped to capitalize. We also felt that if we kept

* From John R. Wooden, *Practical Modern Basketball*, pp. 264–271. Copyright © 1966 The Ronald Press Company, New York.

constant pressure on them they would be forced to "hurry" their offense, which would be in direct contrast to the style of game that they normally played and, perhaps, this would keep them from executing it as well as when they were able to control the tempo.

We used this zone press only after we scored, but the score could be from either the field or the foul line. Since it takes a couple of seconds for the team inbounding the ball to get it and get out-of-bounds into position to inbound it, we usually had time to move to the positions we wanted. As the players became more accustomed to working together, they would make an occasional shift of position without much difficulty. However, I never encouraged this, except in real emergencies, as I felt each individual was physically best suited to play the position to which he was assigned, and an exchange might weaken both positions.

Diagram 1 shows the position to which each man was assigned and how he moved when the ball was inbounded where we wanted it to be.

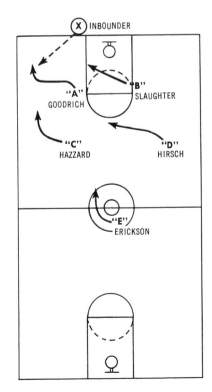

Diagram 1.
UCLA Zone Press

"A"—Goodrich, a left-handed boy with exceedingly quick hands and feet—was assigned to this position. His responsibility was to invite them to pass the ball in to a man in the area indicated by the dotted line. He then advanced on the receiver but was to keep him from driving by on the sideline. If he started to dribble, Goodrich tried to make him stop and turn away where he would be double-teamed by "B" coming over to help. If the receiver did not dribble, Goodrich would advance on him and try to force him to throw a lob or bounce-pass out rather than a crisp straight pass, and he was not to permit him too much time to locate receivers. If the man were able to dribble by him, Goodrich was to turn and chase him and knock the ball on toward a teammate if possible, or double-team him if a teammate slowed down or forced him to stop and turn. Whenever the ball got past him down toward our defensive basket, Goodrich was to hustle back while sizing up the proper place to go.

"B"—Slaughter, a 6-foot 5-inch broad (235-pound) but agile center who runs the 100 in ten seconds—was assigned to this position. He was to discourage the pass to his side and then move over quickly to prevent a return pass to the inbounder in the middle of the floor from the man that Goodrich covered. This was a most important assignment for him. He also was to be alert to two-time with Goodrich in case the man who received the inbound pass started to dribble.

Slaughter's quickness and speed enabled him to play this spot quite well and his size, both his broadness and his height, made him a rather difficult target to pass over or around.

Whenever the ball was moved past his line of defense and down the floor, he was to turn and sprint for the defensive basket, but analyzing the situation while moving.

"C"—Hazzard, a long-armed, quick-handed, aggressive "ball wanter"—was assigned to this position. He was responsible for the area behind Goodrich from the center line to the foul line. He was to stop a driver that might get by Goodrich on that side of the floor and to prevent a receiver from receiving a pass from either the man inbounding the ball or from the man that did receive a short pass from him. He was to inter-

33

cept any lob pass thrown to a receiver in the area for which he was responsible and to cover any receiver of a crisp, straight pass in that area.

"D"—Hirsch, a left-handed, 6-foot 3-inch tough competitor with unusually quick hands—was assigned to this important position. He was responsible for covering the middle of the floor to his left as he faced the inbounder and for the area on his side from the center line to the foul line or deeper in case Slaughter was pulled over. The middle of the floor area between the center circle and the foul circle became an important responsibility for him as soon as the ball was inbounded into the "A" or Goodrich area. The fact that he was left-handed made him more effective in this area from where the pass was likely to come, just as the fact of Goodrich's being left-handed enabled him to fulfill more effectively the assignment in his area. Like "A," "B," and "C," he was to sprint for the defensive end whenever the ball got past his line of defense down the floor and was to size up the situation on his way and take the logical spot.

"E"—Erickson, a very fast and quick, great jumping, 6-foot 5-inch forward with a lot of fire—was to get to the center circle as fast as possible and then direct the defense from there. I considered him our "director" once he got into position and expected the "C" and "D" men to follow his directions. He was responsible for any man who went on down the floor and was expected to intercept any pass that was thrown to any spot in the offensive end if it were thrown from any position as far back as the foul line extended. He was a great defender when outnumbered and always got the ball out quickly to start a fast break. This ability often turned what appeared to be a basket for our opponents into a basket for us. This in turn, sometimes would cause our opponents to become so rattled that we might pick up a few more quick baskets before they could regain their poise and composure.

Some Important Details

The underneath side of the backboard and the net hanging down helped to discourage our opponents from getting the ball in on the "B" side of the floor if they took it out on the "A" side, and our surveys proved that the ball would be inbounded from the "A" side about 90 per cent of the time.

34

However, if they did inbound the ball from the "B" side, the assignments of "A" and "B" were exchanged as were the assignments of "C" and "D."

If they were able to pass the ball in directly from the "A" side to the "B" side, "D" might move up quickly to assume the front responsibility and "B" would move quickly to assume the "D" responsibilities. "A" and "C" would carry out their regular assignments when the ball was inbounded on the side away from them.

An interceptor of any pass in the area of the center of the floor or farther back was to look for Hazzard immediately, and he was to manage to get open. He would drive for the middle of the floor as the side cutting lanes would be filled on the change from defense to offense. Our ability to change quickly from offense to defense often enabled us to capitalize on the errors of our opponents, as we might catch them going the wrong way or with their "heads down."

Goodrich set a successful trap and then sprung it on many occasions by lulling the inbounder into a false sense of security by not molesting the pass in for several times as he would size up the situation. Then he would suddenly move up quickly to make an interception and score an easy basket or heave a pass to a teammate for an easy basket.

The players were taught to "tune in" on Erickson, the director of our press, at all times and to follow his commands without hesitation. It is my firm conviction that it is possible to "tune in" and hear one person, regardless of other noises, if you concentrate on his voice. To be truly effective, this defense must have an "Erickson."

The players were taught not to grab, but to pressure just enough to prevent a straight pass and encourage a lob or bounce pass and still try to prevent the dribble by them. If they dribble, try to direct them into a quick double-team situation.

The importance of breaking back quickly whenever the ball moved by you toward your defensive basket and sizing up the situation as you moved was constantly stressed.

Considerable drill time was used in chasing a man from behind and knocking the ball on toward a teammate who was back. We stressed the no-contact-on-him and the fact that you

35

were not trying to get the ball yourself, but, in a sense, deflecting it on to one of your teammates.

It is necessary to give the players considerable work on the man-to-man press before giving them the zone press. This helps their fundamentals a great deal and will enable them to be that much more effective in the zone press.

If a team is hurting our press too much by quick, clever passing we may go out of the zone press and try a man-to-man press for a while, or change it to a one-three-one, two-one-two, or one-two-one-one zone operated with the same principles.

Additional Facts to Keep in Mind

1. It is a gambling type of defense and requires continued effort and limitless patience if it is to pay dividends.

2. The principal value will probably come from demoralizing the opposition and upsetting their game.

3. It can speed up the game and, perhaps, force an opponent out of their normal style of play.

4. It can cause disharmony and disunity in the opposition.

5. Do not reach in to attempt to take the ball away from an opponent, but play position and force errors when the opponents "hurry." This cuts down fouling and helps to establish the proper philosophy.

6. Try to permit only lob or bounce passes forward. Passes back toward your offensive basket will not hurt you, but crisp passes the least bit forward cause trouble.

7. As soon as the ball passes your individual line of defense, turn and sprint toward your defensive basket and pick up the most dangerous open man. Strong side men should be alive to "two-time" as they go back, and the weak side men should be alert to intercept.

8. All players must be well grounded in the individual defensive fundamentals. I use only a man-to-man pressing defense for our freshman, but use zone principles.

9. If no opponent is in your zone, close in toward the zone that is being attacked.

10. Use tight man-to-man principles if the man in your zone has the ball, and floating man-to-man principles depending upon how far from the ball your man is in the other areas.

11. Results often come in spurts, so apply immediate pressure after acquiring the ball through an error. Often they will try to make up the loss "by hurrying" and will make more errors. Our 1964 team had at least one "spurt" in a period of approximately two minutes in all thirty games in which we outscored our opponents from ten to twenty points. Sometimes it did not come until the middle of the second half, but we would usually have at least one spurt before the end of the first half.

12. The players must realize the necessity and value of and be willing to make the necessary sacrifices to attain and maintain top condition.

13. The players must also be unselfish in regard to scoring as often the scorer when you capitalize will not be the one who caused the error.

14. An outstanding player for the important #5 position is essential. He must be quick, alert, courageous, unselfish, able to "read" the man with the ball, very good at handling the deep defense when outnumbered, a fine rebounder who can get the ball out quickly, very aggressive, with judgment that prevents committing himself too soon, and a player who really loves a challenge.

3
Offense:
How to Shoot

THE PERFECT FREE THROW

NEARLY anyone who uses correct technique and per-
severes through long hours of practice can be a good shooter.
As he practices, the player must also force himself to
concentrate despite the distractions of noise and other
movement on the court. This will eventually become automatic and stand him in good stead when he approaches the
free-throw line during a game, tired, sweaty and assailed by
the yells of excited spectators. Confidence is a key asset in
all forms of shooting—with a gun or a basketball. Players
trying to acquire this quality should be encouraged by the
fact that today many basketball games are won at the foul
line.

A good free-throw shooter is a valuable team man. The
preparatory stance (see Figure 12) shows the body generally
loose, with the knees slightly bent, the right elbow pulled

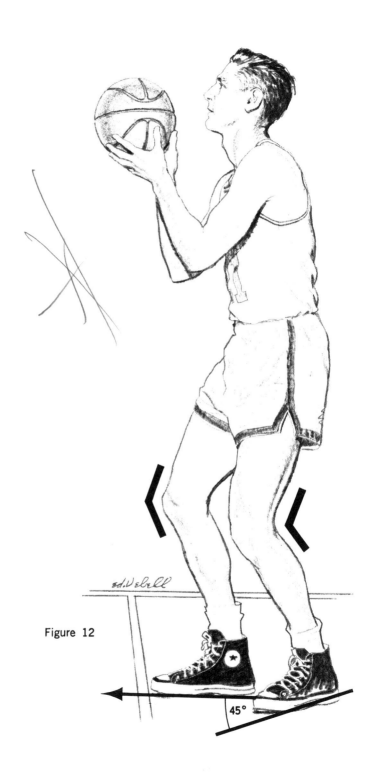

Figure 12

45°

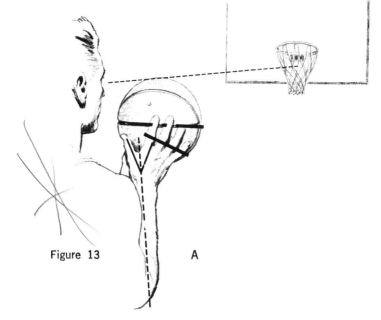

Figure 13   A

A. To prevent the ball from rolling off the side of the hand, the knuckles are at an angle to the seam, not parallel. Aim is at the basket, not the board.

B. Waggling the ball before shooting, loosens the wrists and also gives the "feel" of the ball's weight, which varies with the player's condition.

C. Shooting position, taken after the waggle, has the ball controlled only by the tips of the fingers, where the sense of touch is concentrated.

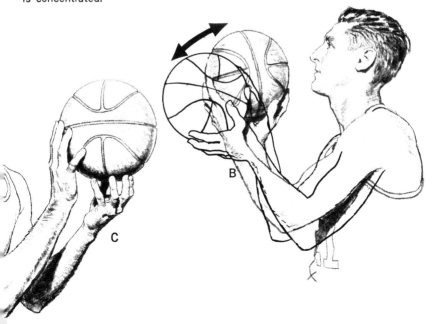

in above the hip for firm control, the right foot pointed at the basket, the left foot at a 45-degree angle. The position is taken after a deep breath and a pause to relax from game tension. At this time the ball is held with both hands and raised to the level for sighting over the top, the ball obscuring most of the net, as shown in Figure 13.

In Figure 14A, numbers 1 to 4 show smooth, single-motion windup. Between 4 and 5, the ball is brought back and the wrist is cocked. Then thrust begins in the legs, moves up through the body as the arm is extended, and push is imparted by the sum total of these forces. The ball is not thrown. It is propelled by precisely the same flow of power as in putting the shot. The feet do not leave the floor, so balance is maintained. At the instant of release, the ball should roll off only three fingers if it is held properly (see Figure 13C, page 41). These are the thumb, index and middle fingers. Soft trajectory and back spin help the ball "sit" on rim if it hits, rather than bounce off wildly.

Follow-through is just as essential as in golf or baseball swing. If the free-throw motion is smooth, follow-through flows naturally. In Figure 14B, the arm is fully extended and in a straight line. The wrist is still at the same angle as in the first step. Eyes never leave the basket. Most players use this type of free throw because it is virtually the same in most essentials as the one-hand jump, so a player practices one while executing the other.

THE BASIC SHOTS

Winning basketball is the result of scoring points—which means shooting of one kind or another. There are many different styles and theories of shooting, and wide areas of disagreement among players and coaches about how to make particular shots. A player is influenced by what serves him best; a coach is influenced by the methods of his successful players. Shooting is a highly personal skill. Nevertheless, there

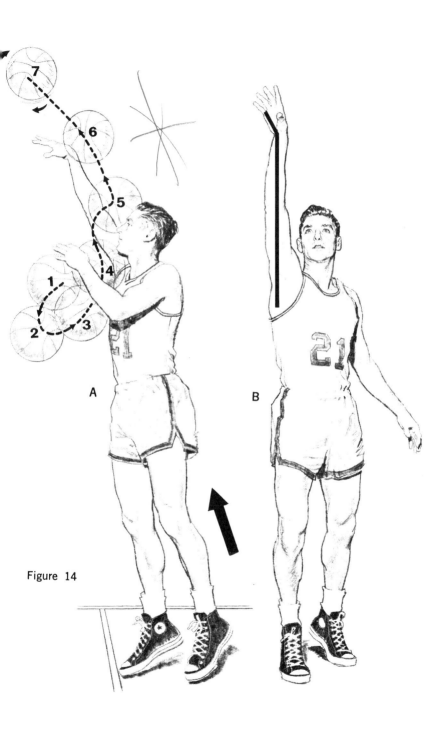

Figure 14

are also wide areas of agreement on certain fundamental practices. For example, even the casual spectator will note that most of the pro game's high scorers release the ball quickly, to cut down a defender's chances of blocking the ball or obscuring the shooter's vision. On the other hand, a perennial high scorer may actually be a relatively poor shooter, but he is so expert at feinting his defender out of position that he gets more time and space for his shots than many other players.

Every good shooter follows through on all his shots. Every good shooter keeps his eye on the target, not the ball. Except for a Wilt Chamberlain, who simply overwhelms his opposition, a good shooter develops a variety of shots and learns to shoot well with either hand. This prevents the defense from anticipating his moves and making it more difficult for him to shoot. There is no question but that the soft shot with a gentle arch has the best chance of, first, going through the hoop and, second, bouncing in if it hits the rim. Yet a few of the sport's better shooters, like Jerry West, still fire the ball hard, on a flat line toward the basket. Nearly all good shooters aim for the basket, not the backboard, except on layups.

In addition to all this, players are constantly developing new shots and variations on old ones—either under the stress of the moment in a game or through long hours of practice. No shot catalogue is really complete. On the following pages, however, an arsenal of the basics is shown, and methods of using the shots are discussed.

The Layup

This is generally conceded to be the easiest shot in the game, yet also one of the most important. The object of a fast break, which every team uses when it can and which many teams try to use all the time, is to send one player, unguarded, in for a layup. The object of many set plays is the same. Despite this, the shot is often missed, after all the effort that has gone into setting it up, because the

44

Figure 15
The layup

player with the ball is usually moving swiftly and is the object of much cheering and yelling from spectators who are delighted or dismayed (depending on which team they are supporting) by the spectacle of two easy points.

There is considerable difference of opinion on the execution of a few of the fundamentals. Some experts believe that all layups should be banked off the backboard; some believe that layups from the side should be banked but that those made from directly in front of the basket should be aimed to drop in over the rim; a few hold that all layups should be shot cleanly, ignoring the backboard.

On the subject of putting spin on the ball, there is also disagreement. Certainly, if the ball is simply banked off the backboard without spin, it is possible to achieve a softer shot. The most intelligent approach for a player or a coach is to decide precisely what method to use—bank or not, spin or not—and stick to it. Under game conditions, a player should not have to decide such matters; the shot should become automatic, instinctive, like most successful maneuvers. Only when he is closely guarded and is still obliged to attempt a layup should a player have to improvise details of the shot.

It is best if a player has sufficient skill with both hands so that he can shoot a layup with his left hand when approaching the basket from that side, and with his right hand from the right side. However, regardless of which hand is used to shoot, the player should push off from the floor with the opposite foot and strive for maximum height. He should hold the ball in both hands, over his head, until he reaches the highest point of his leap, then release it with the proper hand, laying it up against the backboard or over the rim as softly as possible. The ball should be held and released by the fingertips—not the palms. The shooter should keep his eyes glued on the target, not the ball, during his approach and the follow-through.

With the arrival of big men like Wilt Chamberlain and Lew Alcindor on the scene, we now have the stuff shot. The shooter seems to jump barely inches from the floor as he reaches up with both hands and stuffs the ball through the hoop. It's almost unstoppable.

46

The Hook Shot

The great advantage of this shot, especially today when shot-blocking is all the rage, is the fact that it is almost impossible to block when executed reasonably correctly, especially by someone like Lew Alcindor. The great drawback of the hook is that it is a very difficult maneuver. It requires utmost precision and concentration, which must be acquired through long practice hours. But just as important as the mechanics of the shot itself is the shooter's ability to get into the proper position—to receive the ball and then shoot. He must learn what the best positions are for him, and how to maneuver his defending player so that he can get into position at the right time. Few hook-shooters have ever perfected the shot so that it is effective at any real distance from the basket. The limit for most is around foul-line length of an arc around the backboard.

The shooter starts with his back to the basket, holding the ball in both hands, and with his defender behind him. He should keep the bulk of his body between the defender and the ball until he shoots, and then he should raise his free arm, elbow bent, to further protect the ball. Obviously, it is extremely valuable for a hooker to develop efficiency with both hands, so that the defender cannot ignore feints in either direction. The shot can be made, after a feint or two, from this standing position or after a step away from the basket with either foot. If the step or the pivot is made with the left foot, the shot is made with the right hand, and vice versa. The ball is released, with the arm fully extended, from the fingertips, as with all other shots. As the ball is crossed over the body in preparation for shooting, the shooter turns his head and fixes his eyes on the backboard spot he intends to hit, or just above the rim if he is shooting from in front of the basket. He concentrates on this spot through the shot and the follow-through, directing the ball by feel, not sight.

Figure 16
The hook shot

A side benefit of the hook is that the shot is easily converted to a pass at the last moment if the would-be shooter spots a free teammate under the basket.

The Jump Shot

Today, more shots are taken from the jumping position than from any other. Some players shoot nothing but jump shots. Because this shot is so widely used, a great variety of styles have developed, each best suited to the player who uses it. Many players use almost exactly the same technique for their free throws as they use for the jumper; a few, like Hal Greer, actually use the jumper at the free-throw line, though they don't jump quite so high there as they do in shooting from the field.

The jump-shooter is usually so successful in avoiding the blocking attempts of his defender—this is one of the big advantages of the shot—that he is often shocked when it is blocked in a game. Almost always, this occurs because the shooter has not tried to feint the defender into committing himself beforehand. Every really good jump-shooter practices some deceptive moves just as hard as he practices his shooting. A feint with the head, eyes or hands—just enough to get the defender up on his toes—is usually enough to insure that the shot will not be blocked. When the defender starts down from his toes to regain proper balance, the shooter begins his leap—and he literally has the jump on the defender.

From this point, individual style takes over, but there are a number of general rules. The ball should be held in both hands until the moment of shooting, for protection and control. It should be held and shot from the fingertips, not the palms, with the wrist flexible and the shooting arm fully extended. As always, the follow-through is essential— the eyes still fixed on the target, the arm still fully extended. Most players get best results if they release the ball at the instant they achieve maximum height. A few, however, have such marvelous body control that they are able to shoot from nearly any point during the leap. Among today's players, Earl Monroe and Walt Frazier are two examples.

Figure 17
The jump shot

Once again, the question of bank shot vs. clean shot arises. Beginners especially are far better off ignoring the backboard, as backboards vary considerably from court to court, in material, in resilience, in size. Some have dead spots, some are fixed, some suspended. Trying for the clean shot permits the shooter to discount such variations.

The Overhead Set Shot

The two-hand, so-called chest shot used to be the standard shot in basketball. It is still seen, of course, and it is possible that there may be a wide revival of its use because of the current prevalence of zone defenses in college and high school play. These defenses make it extremely difficult for the offensive team to penetrate close to the basket and

Figure 18
The overhead set shot

therefore place a premium on good outside shooting. However, few players today learn the chest shot, preferring the one-hand or two-hand jumper. Some use the overhead shot, and most of the fundamentals are the same for this as for the chest shot.

In assuming proper position for the shot, a good guide is whatever is most comfortable for each player, but there are a few generally applicable rules. The feet should be roughly the player's shoulder width apart, one a bit ahead of the other, with the weight slightly forward. Practice will determine for each player how much his knees should be flexed in relation to the distance of the shot—the longer the distance, the greater the flexing. In the chest shot, the elbows should be tucked in close to the body, not flapping loosely; in the overhead, the arms should be almost fully extended. The ball should be held loosely and, as always, with the fingertips.

A trick that good players learn early is to receive passes with the fingertips. Then they are always ready to shoot, without having to shift the ball around in their hands. The reason fingertips are used is that they are far more sensitive than the palms and also afford better control.

A common mistake by beginners from this point on is to push the ball toward the basket. Instead, the following is what should take place. The knees are flexed to gain some of the power that will eventually send the ball on its way. At the lowest point of the flexing, the wrists are unlocked. Then, simultaneously, the knees are straightened, the wrists are snapped and the player rises just a bit from the floor. The wrist and finger action will give the ball reverse spin, which helps soften the shot. All this time, the shooter's eyes never leave the spot just over the front rim—his target. And in the follow-through, he still sights through his arms, extended in direct line with the shot.

4
Offense:
Other Basics

ONE–ON–ONE

IT is not a bad idea to start practice sessions with the drill in which one offensive man tries to outmaneuver one defensive man. The one-on-one is particularly valuable at the beginning of a season because it allows the coach to spot several important things about the offensive player: his ability to keep the ball away from the opponent, his strong or weak points in head and body fakes. If there are weaknesses they can be corrected so that later—under game conditions—he will be able to free himself from the enemy defender to drive for the basket or to feed a pass to a teammate.

In the drawings on pages 54–69 the offensive men are in black uniforms and the defensive men are in white uniforms.

Figure 19   A

A. The player protects the ball while he decides which maneuver will best deceive the defender and open the way toward the basket.

B. Head-and-shoulder fake to left causes the defensive man to slide to his own right. The ball is held low in order to begin the dribble.

C. The offensive player starts to drive off his right foot as the defender, fooled by the fake, is off balance and so cannot recover in time.

D. The driving player has his left hand and shoulder protecting the ball and is already a half step beyond the re-covering defender.

54

B

C

D

Figure 20   A

A. To begin this maneuver, the forward loops a pass in to the pivot man, who comes out to meet the ball and stands fast.

B. The forward fakes to his left, then goes to his right as the defender backs up, trying to anticipate the direction of the play.

ONE-ON-ONE WITH PIVOT

Players should learn how to run the defender into a block (also referred to as a pick) that renders him helpless. On offense are a forward and a pivot man. Their aim is to take the forward's defender out of the play. In Figure 20, note that the pivot man does not move once he has the ball. This opportunity arises many times during a game, and two smart offensive players can execute the maneuver quickly and work a man loose for a basket before the defender knows what is happening to him.

56

B

C

C. The pivot man protects the ball as the forward moves toward it. The defender is forced into the block and is unable to follow.

D. The pivot man hands off to the cutting forward, who is now free, as the defender cannot get around the block in time.

D

Figure 21   A

A. The ball has been passed to the pivot man. The offensive man in the rear starts to move (arrow), forcing the defender to back up.

COMBATING THE "STICK"

There are only two things an individual defender can do to combat a block or pick. One is to stick with the offensive man and follow him no matter where he goes. The alternative is to switch guarding assignments when the man he is defending runs him into a block. In the situation shown in Figure 21, the defense tries to stick, but the offense still maneuvers it out of position.

58

CAMROSE LUTHERAN COLLEGE
LIBRARY

B. As soon as the defender starts backing up, the other offensive man begins cutting in toward the pivot, who fakes a pass.

B

C

C. Defensive man No. 2 tries to stick with the cutter, who now stops, setting up the block for his waiting teammate (No. 5).

D. The cutter's teammate (No. 5) now comes around the block easily, having gotten a step ahead of his defender with the earlier fake.

E. The pivot man hands the ball off to teammate No. 5, who is now completely free as his defender is blocked out of the play.

D

E

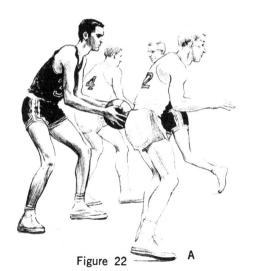

Figure 22   A

A. Pivot man takes the pass and waits for his teammates to cross in front. The offensive man in the rear first fakes the defender toward basket.

B. Defender No. 2 moves with offensive man No. 1 and bumps into the pivot, while offensive man No. 5 swings the defender wide.

C. Blocked out, No. 2 calls "switch," but the wide arc of offensive man No. 5 makes the defense switch very difficult to execute.

D. Although the defenders have switched their assignments, No. 4 has been taken out of play and offensive man No. 1 is free.

COMBATING THE "SWITCH"

The defensive players often try to avoid being blocked out by switching their guarding assignments. In Figure 22, the defenders switch assignments, but the offense maneuvers them into a mistake with the help of the pivot man. The maneuver looks simple but must be executed swiftly and accurately to be successful.

B

C

D

WEAK–SIDE PLAY

All of the fundamental maneuvers shown on the previous pages are combined in what is known as weak-side play, so-called because the side of the court on which the offense concentrates most of its men is known as the strong side. In Figure 23, the key to the play's effectiveness lies in fooling defensive man No. 2 long enough for offensive man No. 5 to get a step ahead of him on the weak side. This clears him for a pass and a drive-in for an easy layup. The play begins with the offensive team's two guards bringing the ball downcourt. Pick it up at the first drawing.

A

Figure 23

A. One offensive guard dribbles in front of the other, and the two exchange sides of the court as the defense switches assignments.

B

B. One guard (No. 5) continues toward the near side of the court (foreground), thus forcing the defense to spread itself wide.

C

C. As the man with the ball prepares to pass, defender No. 2 watches him (for possible interception) but also keeps an eye on No. 5.

D

D. The offense's left forward moves up from the corner to take the pass and, the instant it is thrown, No. 5 starts to cut toward the basket. Defender No. 2, who has kept one eye on the strong side, is trapped. He cannot intercept or recover in time to catch No. 5.

E. As soon as the forward has received the pass, he whirls toward No. 5 who is cutting down the weak side of the court at top speed.

E

F

F. Defender No. 2, realizing that he is trapped, tries to back up fast enough to block the forward's pass, which he knows is coming.

G. No. 2 cannot block the pass, and none of his defensive teammates can help him because they are all on the strong side.

H. The guard goes in for an easy layup as other offensive teammates move in for the rebound, just in case the shot is missed.

68

G

H

5
Offense:
How to Work
the Shuffle

MANY teams have had success using an offense that can best be described as the shuffle, a highly disciplined style of play, as opposed to the wide-open, run-and-shoot variety. As such, it requires a coach who is a good teacher and intelligent players who dedicate themselves to team play rather than individual heroics. Like all first-rate systems, it is actually very simple, but, to be successful, it demands perfect execution of its simple details. It has the weakness—if this is a weakness—of requiring at least reasonably good ball-handling on the part of every player on the floor. The fact is, however, that every player, regardless of what special skill enables him to make his team, should master the fundamentals of ball-handling.

And the shuffle's advantages far outweigh the minor drawbacks. Nothing upsets a team more than the sight of its rival effectively executing simple plays with cool, machine-like precision, ignoring temporary failures and sticking to its

71

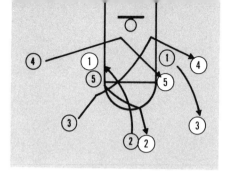

Diagram 2

prearranged plans. The shuffle enables five players of only average physical qualifications to beat a team that may be taller, shoot better and run faster but doesn't use its collective head and plays like a bunch of individual stars. Its reliance on team play also works, automatically, toward good team spirit.

The shuffle operates from two basic formations: the so-called "overload left" (the gray circles shown in Diagram 2), and the "overload right" (the white circles). If a play that starts from "overload left" does not result in a good shot, all of the players will have filled similar positions on the right side of the court and can continue with another play from there. This continuous flow of movement—almost perpetual motion—gives the defense very little time to set itself.

A

Figure 24

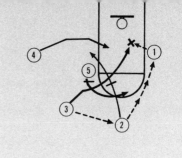

Diagram 3

THE BASIC PATTERN

In the shuffle, any player can take any one of the five spots numbered in Diagram 3. No one plays forward, guard or center all the time, so everyone must know the moves required for each position. A trademark of the shuffle is the quick, direct pass that insures ball control and forces the defense to cover a wider area, thus increasing the chance of freeing someone for an easy shot. At its best, as shown here, the shuffle increases the possibility of surprise by requiring almost no dribbling. (The numbers on the players' shirts in Figures 24–27 correspond to those used in Diagrams 3–6.)

A. This short pass from the 3-man to the 2-man is the start of the basic pattern from which six plays can be run, every one of them looking the same to the defense until the last second—when it is too late.

B.

B. No. 2 quickly relays No. 3's pass to No. 1, as 3 begins his drive for the basket. He starts out by running, under control, toward No. 5, while checking the position of his defensive opponent, whom he hopes to back into No. 5.

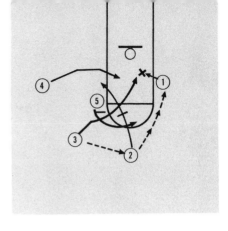

Diagram 3

C. His guard successfully blocked to the outside, No. 3 cuts inside and drives hard for the basket. If No. 3's guard had backed to No. 5's left instead and wound up in the lane, No. 3 would have cut outside No. 5. If No. 3's guard had stayed with him, the play would change; someone other than 3 would take the shot.

C

D

D. No. 3 continues at full speed to keep his advantage over No. 5's guard, who has abandoned 5 upon realizing that the free-throw lane is suddenly open. No. 1, noting that No. 3 has successfully gained clear access to the basket, immediately relays No. 2's pass.

E. The lay-up results. No. 4 moves in for a possible rebound. If No. 3 had been well guarded, No. 1 could have shot or passed to No. 5, who is free to shoot from just behind the foul line (see Diagram 3). If everything failed, the play would have continued from an overload right.

Diagram 3

E

A QUICK OPTION

By presenting a constant scoring threat from all five players, the shuffle gains several important advantages: it never lets the defense rest or double-team one player easily, because all five must be constantly guarded. Its fast but simple pass patterns can force a man-to-man defense into areas the defense does not wish to occupy, resulting in either a free offensive man or a foul. In Figure 25, note that the passing in this play, another in the series from the third option, follows the same 3-2-1 sequence as in the previous play, and that everyone starts running the very same routes.

A

Figure 25

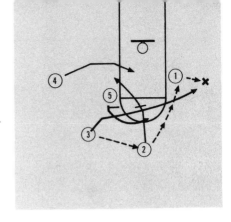

Diagram 4

A. The 3-man has again cut inside the 5-man, causing the defense to think he is again going straight down the free-throw lane. But, seeing that his guard (No. 24) is dropping back into the lane, No. 3 cuts sharply to his right and moves above the 1-man, who has received No. 2's pass.

79

B. No. 3's sudden shift has led his guard into a block by No. 1. However, if 3 is still covered, No. 1 can either feed No. 4, pass to No. 5 (see diagram) or, by dribbling out a few steps, can set up an overload right formation and start an entirely new play.

C. No. 3 shoots over a protective screen formed by No. 1, who is rolling toward the basket for a rebound. As shown by the players' final positions on the diagram, the 1- 2- and 4-men are all in excellent position for a rebound.

B

Diagram 4

C

CREATING AN OUTSIDE THREAT

The shuffle does have its drawbacks. Too much pattern movement can discourage players from free-lancing or using the fast break, both of which are desirable. Also, running from the overload left or right formation can overcrowd one side of the floor and jam the play. Yet despite these dangers and its seeming repetition, the shuffle has marvelous versatility, as shown here in Figure 26, another play from the third option. It presents one of the many alternatives available to the 1-man once he has received the usual pass from the 2-man.

Figure 26   A

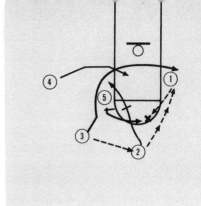

Diagram 5

A. The two basic moves in the shuffle (gray lines in Diagram 5), are the cut by the 3-man and the roll by No. 5. When the defense sinks back to crowd No. 3, who was the shooter on the first two plays, 3 becomes a decoy instead. He has again drawn No. 5's guard into the lane, leaving 5 free as the defense reacts to the expected pass to No. 3.

B

B. The team's best shooter is occupy-
ing the 5-spot for this play. Like all
four of his teammates, he duplicates
the exact moves of the first two plays
—until the 1-man omits the usual pass
to No. 3, who has gone by him. Instead,
No. 1 passes to No. 5 who, at this
point in the third option, is almost
always in the open.

C. The 2-man sets up the same screen
that kept No. 5 free on the first two
plays, and 5 takes an easy jump shot.
Thus, on all three plays, the 1-man has
been able to outmaneuver the defense
at the very last second. He has the
option of shooting, feeding 3, 5 or 4,
or dribbling out a few steps to start a
new play.

Diagram 5

Figure 27

A

TO FOIL A SWITCH

Because players in the shuffle are constantly changing positions, the defense has difficulty finding a weak spot. Even an average shooter becomes a scoring threat. The defense is further confused in spotting the potential scorer because the shooter does not get the ball until he enters the shooting area. Thus there is no indication of which player is being set up until the shot is taken, as shown in Figure 27, a play from the fourth option, used to combat a switching defense.

B

Diagram 6

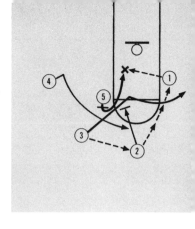

A. The play starts with the 5-man facing the basket as he blocks for 3, who cuts deeper than usual to lure away 5's guard (No. 35), who switches to No. 3 when he sees that 3's guard has been blocked by 5. The 3-man then cuts sharply to his right to draw his new guard (No. 35) out of the lane. As Diagram 6 shows, the lane is further cleared because the 4-man has changed his usual course and is drawing his guard up above the free-throw line.

B. By facing the basket before No. 3's guard switched to him, No. 5 automatically gained a full-step advantage. He keeps it by moving quickly down the empty lane for a pass from No. 1. The lane was open because each man drew his guard from the shooting area.

6
A Tribute to
Bob Cousy

IN a game that is apparently dominated by extremely tall men and in which an athlete may succeed just by doing one thing well—say shooting—it is still true that one of the finest players yet produced is only a bit over average height and has deliberately mastered every facet of his sport. He is Bob Cousy, 6 feet 1 inch tall, 185 pounds. His remarkable success should be an inspiration to every youngster who wants to play the game, and the methods he used are in themselves a guidebook to stardom. The keys to Cousy's achievements were versatility and imagination. For years he was not only one of the game's highest scorers, but its best playmaker and a leader in assists. This simply means that far from being a self-seeking individualist on the court, he was the perfect team player in a game which, above all, demands cooperative effort.

It is especially significant that Cousy first came to the attention of his high school coach because he was seemingly ambidextrous. Actually, he is right-handed, as most of us are. But even as a youngster, Cousy was well aware that in basketball it is tremendously important to be able to do nearly everything equally well with both hands. Here's the way he puts it: "The primary skill a young player must try to acquire is to master his weak hand, his left hand if he is a righty. Learning to shoot with it amounts to only a small advance. To be a true threat, a man must be able to move equally well to his left and right and this includes being able to dribble, pass and shoot while going in both directions. The whole art of dribbling, for instance, depends on keeping your body between the ball and the man guarding you. Against a capable opponent, you cannot drive forward from left to right, say, unless you can dribble with your left hand. Otherwise the ball is unprotected."

Further on the subject of versatility, Cousy says: "Unless he also possesses an accurate shot, an agile dribbler can operate only at 50 percent of his effectiveness. If he is no threat shooting from the outside, his man can afford to give him room and let him shoot, gambling that he will make a poor percentage of his shots. By giving him this room, the defensive man acquires a margin for error which allows him to stay between his man and the basket even if he has been slightly faked out of position or has anticipated a move incorrectly. The key to offensive play for a maturing player is enlarging his number of moves, his variety of shots. Just as a good pitcher in baseball throws every pitch with the same motion, a good basketball player begins all of his moves from the same position, the better to confuse the defense."

It is interesting to note that one of the sport's brightest stars, Jerry West, testifies to the value of this same key ingredient. West, like Cousy, was an All America player in college. He explains his rapid development as a professional this way: "I can do a lot more with the ball now. I was strictly a right-handed shot and I didn't drive much, so the defense was playing me a whole step to the right and in tight. Now I can go to my left and shoot with my left hand, and I'm driving a lot. The driving has helped a great deal.

I don't have hands in my face every time I go up for a jump shot, and I'm getting five or six more foul shots a game."

Cousy, like Jerry West, Walt Frazier, Pete Maravich and all other versatile players, acquired most of his arsenal of skills through long hours of practice. He was fascinated by what he could learn and, clearly, was dedicated to the game—another guide to success in any field. "To me," he says, "practice was never work. It was and is time spent at the thing I love best. It gives me a chance to improvise, to create. Maybe I shouldn't put it on such a high plane, but it does give a player a chance to dream up new things and to polish them, and that is one of the reasons why the game has always had such a tremendous appeal for me."

Actually, Cousy's most famous maneuver (the behind-the-back dribble, shown on pages 92–93) was not something he dreamed up during practice. It came to him in the heat of a college game, as a way out of a difficult situation. And this was the second key to his greatness—his imagination, his ability to come up with something new, right on the court, when it was required.

Few players had Cousy's creativity, and it is difficult, if not impossible, to acquire. But the quality that drove him to improvise, to find new ways of getting the job done, is the unfailing mark of all great athletes—the unquenchable desire to win. Playing hundreds of basketball games over nearly twenty years of competition, Cousy still wanted to win each game so badly that he began to prepare himself, mentally, several hours before tipoff time, concentrating on the problems he and his team would face. In the dressing room before the game, his normally expressive brown eyes began to lose their animation and a sort of glaze tightened his mobile face. He became quiet and solemn and, in fact, somewhat drowsy. Part of this was natural. He had every fine athlete's capacity to relax at hard moments. But part of it was calculated. He wanted to play each game up to the

Figure 28

Cousy executes his behind-the-back dribble at full tilt. This sequence shows him changing his direction abruptly.

hilt, and this helped him collect his energy and shape his concentration.

Once on the floor, he changed considerably. A tremendous, burning desire came over him. He poured so much of himself into the game that his absorption temporarily suffused the rest of his personality. He was instantly aware of the rival team's mistakes and exploited them brilliantly and relentlessly, his passwork, for example, nearly always evoked gasps of surprise from spectators, just as Maravich does today. Many observers, indeed, expressed the belief that it was probably very difficult for Cousy's teammates to keep up with him, to know what he'd be doing next. The truth was just the reverse. Cousy's passes were sure and precise and were made at exactly the right moment, even if

92

E   F   G   H

they were delivered in an unorthodox manner and from an apparently "impossible" position. "When someone else passes you the ball," a teammate of Cousy's once said, "very often there's nothing you can do with it except eat it. When Cousy passes you the ball, there's always a reason."

Cousy first performed his most distinctive maneuver in 1949, as a player for Holy Cross, in a game with Loyola of Chicago. There were ten seconds to go and Cousy was driving hard for the basket, hoping for a layup or a close-in shot. But he could not shake his defender, Loyola's Ralph Klaerich, who was a fraction of a step ahead of Cousy and overplaying him to his right side. Klaerich was ready to block any shot Cousy might try as he finished his dribble. But Cousy finished the dribble somewhat differently from the way Klaerich—or, for that matter, Cousy or anyone else—

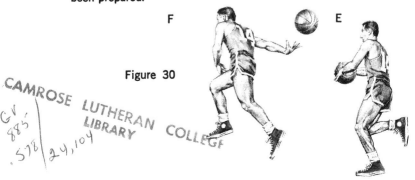

Figure 29

The behind-the-back transfer was a Cousy exclusive. When he whipped the ball behind his back with his right hand, on some occasions, the defensive man, anticipating that Cousy would get off a pass, shifted to cover the whole play. Cousy, as in this right-to-left sequence, would then complete the behind-the-back transfer from his right hand to his left, and, with the way open, lay up the shot himself.

was expecting. Cousy reached behind his back with his right hand and slapped the ball to the floor, found the ball with his left hand as it came up on the bounce to his left side, and then, without a break in stride or dribble, drove to the left, leaped into the air and sank a left-hander that won the game.

"People said that I had been practicing the dribble," Cousy recalls, "but I had never even thought of it until the

The double transfer was used if the defensive man between Cousy and the basket elected to stay with Cousy and so leave one of the other Celtics unguarded. On completing his first around-the-back transfer, Cousy brought the ball around a second time with his left hand and passed to the free man. Such moves required discretion; he could not overdo them or the defense would have been prepared.

Figure 30

CAMROSE LUTHERAN COLLEGE
GV
885
.S78 24,104

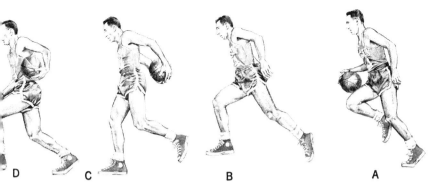

D   C   B   A

moment the situation forced me into it. I was absolutely amazed myself at what I had done. It was only much later that I began to practice it so that I could make it a reliable part of my repertoire."

Figure 29 depicts this famous improvisation step by step. The model for the drawings, of course, is Bob Cousy.

Cousy's team value was based solidly on his skill as a playmaker. His sleight-of-hand tricks, far from being empty show-boating as was the case with many of his imitators, were brilliant, functional basketball. Equipped with a fine sense of pattern and superb reflexes, he also had peripheral vision, which enabled him to see not only the men in front of him but a full 180-degree angle of the action. Thus, he could open up a seemingly clogged court by appearing to focus in one direction, simultaneously spotting an apparently unreachable teammate in another area, and quickly turning him into a scoring threat with a whiplash pass. There was implicit deception in Cousy's straight basketball, which is the secret of any great player's success, and it was only in those exceptional circumstances when extra measures pay off soundly that he resorted to his really fancy stuff.

C   B   A

His backhand pass, the simple maneuver illustrated in Figure 31, is one that Cousy used for years with teammate Bill Sharman on the Boston Celtics—with astonishing success. As with all such simple moves, any player can learn it, but it will not be successful unless the passer and the receiver operate with perfect timing. The object is to give the receiver a split-second extra time to get off a shot. If that doesn't work, the stage is set for a quick give-and-go play, with the passer breaking clear, taking the return pass and then making the shot himself.

The backhand pass was one maneuver Cousy often used when, leading a 3-on-2 attack, he reached the foul-line area and found his route to the basket blocked by a defensive player. As this sequence shows (from right to left), he flipped the ball in mid-dribble to a trailing teammate cutting behind him, then either cut for a return pass or simply stopped dead to set up a screen for the teammate.

C   B   A

Figure 31